Sailing

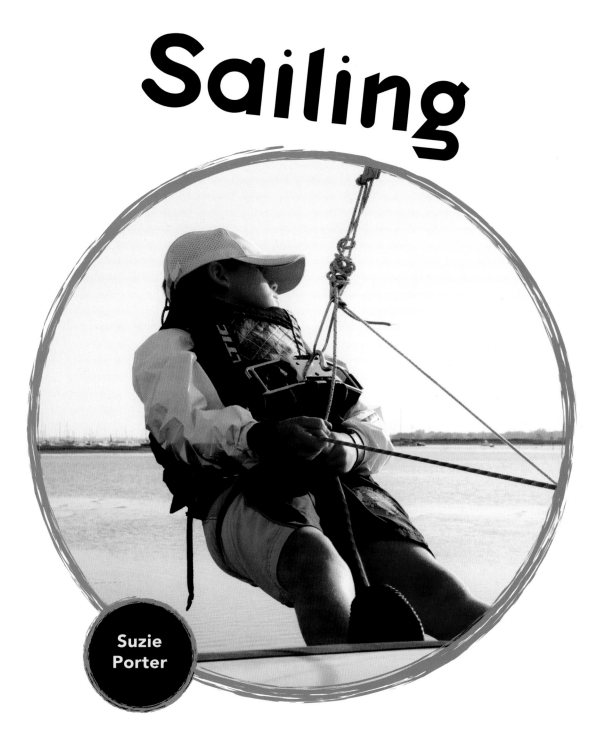

Suzie Porter

PowerKiDS press.

New York

Published in 2011 by The Rosen Publishing Group Inc.
29 East 21st Street, New York, NY 10010

Copyright © 2011 Wayland/
The Rosen Publishing Group, Inc.

First Edition

Senior Editor: Debbie Foy
Designer: Rebecca Painter
Photographer: Michael Wicks
Photoshoot Coordinator: Jon Richards

Library of Congress Cataloging-in-Publication Data

Porter, Suzie.
Sailing / by Suzie Porter. — 1st ed.
     p. cm. — (Get outdoors)
Includes index.
ISBN 978-1-4488-3297-2 (library binding)
1. Sailing. I. Title.
GV811.P67 2011
797.1'24—dc22
                                    2010024355

Photographs:
The author and publisher would like to thank the following people for participating in our photoshoot: Lucy Scott, Eve Townsend, and Ben Townsend.

All photography by Michael Wicks except
4 Dreamstime.com/Dwight Smith; 7 top Wang Song/Xinhua Press/Corbis
26 Dreamstime.com/Ahmad Faizal Yahya; 28 Getty/Alison Langley;
29 Dreamstime.com/Gabigarcia

Manufactured in China
CPSIA Compliance Information: Batch #WAW1102PK: For Further Information
contact Rosen Publishing, New York, New York at 1-800-237-9932

Contents

What Is Sailing? 4

Why Go Sailing? 6

How to Get Started 8

Sailing Equipment 10

Understanding the Wind 12

Getting Afloat 14

Changing Direction 16

Making a Turn 18

In Deep Water! 20

The Next Step 22

On the Open Water 24

Competition Racing 26

Sailing Challenges! 28

Glossary 30

Further Reading and Web Sites . . 31

Index 32

What is Sailing?

Sailing is a sport for everyone—no matter what their age or ability. A day on the water can mean anything from a family trip on the river to serious racing on the ocean. Once you know the basics, there are endless possibilities for sailing fun!

The Basics of Sailing

Using a sail to catch the wind, a boat is propelled through the water as fast as the wind can carry it. Since the wind affects how fast you go, you can use the sail to speed up, slow down, and change direction. The **rudder** is also used to control the direction that the boat sails in, and works something like a steering wheel does in a car.

77

Freedom on the water! Sailing boats come in many different shapes and sizes, with up to three sails.

Sailing in the Past

A traditional sailing **dinghy** was originally made from wood with a simple cotton sail. They were used for travel across rivers and fishing in shallow waters. Although wooden boats are still used today for cruising trips and family days out, they are heavy and not as fast or strong as today's lighter-weight boats that many people now enjoy racing. The fastest boats are the lightest, so most dinghies are now made from strong, light plastics.

In the past, sailing boats were made from wood and had cotton sails.

Types of Sailing Boats

Yachts are the largest types of boats, and can be used to sleep on or even live on. Dinghies are smaller and easier to manage, so most sailors learn how to sail in them. A dinghy can be **launched** and **recovered** from the water each time you use it, and is kept on a **trailer** on the land so is easy to move around and store. Dinghies typically only have one or two sails and space for one or two sailors, making them perfect for learning to sail with a friend or on your own. Boats with just one sail and space for one sailor are known as single-handed, and boats with an extra sail and space for two sailors are known as double-handed.

*In a single-handed (one-person) dinghy, the sailor controls the sail and steers the boat, so they are called the **helm**. The second sailor onboard a double-handed (two-person) boat controls the second extra sail, and is called the **crew**.*

Why Go Sailing?

If you're looking for a new sports challenge and enjoy being around water, look no further than sailing! Although being afloat might take a little getting used to, before the end of your first day on the water, you will be confident enough to go sailing on your own.

Physical and Mental Skills

Setting off on your first sailing adventure is an exhilarating and rewarding experience since you have to work on balance, control, concentration, and other skills to speed through the water.

Sailing requires determination, skilled boat handling, and confidence. Once you are happy with the basics, you will find yourself eager to try out other adventures on the water. Sailing is a challenging activity and you will never be bored. In fact, after just one session, you will probably be hooked!

Just for Fun

Sailing is the ideal way to get outdoors and be active without having to plan ahead too much. Sailing takes place anywhere that there is enough water to float a boat, including lakes, rivers, streams, and oceans, so you can be sure that there will be a sailing club, school, or training center just down the road from you.

After a couple of lessons, you will be able to go on cruising adventures with your friends and family to discover new beaches and locations that you have never seen before.

Sailing is the perfect way to enjoy the outdoors with a group of friends at a local sailing club.

Going for Gold

Although many people sail just for fun, some sailors enjoy adding a competitive edge to the sport. Dinghy racing takes place all over the country, and at every level, from local sailing club competitions to big international events.

The Olympic Games gathers together the very best sailors in the world to race against each other. Competitive sailing is not just about skills on the water, but also fitness, strength, stamina, and racing tactics.

With three gold medal successes, Ben Ainslie is the most successful Olympic sailor of all time.

Warming Up

Before you go sailing, it is important to warm up your arms and legs, because you will be working these muscles hard. Pulling in the sails and leaning out of the boat to keep it as balanced as possible will put a lot of strain on your arm, stomach, and thigh muscles.

Good warm-ups to run through include a gentle jog, making big circles with your arms to get the blood pumping, and squats and star jumps to get your legs ready to work.

How to Get Started

Anyone who enjoys being active and taking on a new challenge will enjoy the exhilaration that comes with single-handed or double-handed sailing. Start your sailing career in a responsible way by learning the techniques and safety advice from professionals. Ideally, you should also be able to swim at least 165 ft. (50 m).

First Time Afloat

The best time to learn sailing is during the summer months when the weather and the water are relatively warm. Unlike indoors sports, sailing is reliant on the weather. You need wind to move the boat and clear skies to keep you warm. Although getting wet when sailing is inevitable, rainy conditions will make you cold and reduce visibility on the water, running the risk of accidents.

Always learn from a qualified instructor at a local sailing club. This way you will learn correct techniques and safety advice.

Trying the Ropes

Before you splash out on your own equipment, a taster session is a good way to make sure you enjoy sailing. Clubs and sailing centers offer short courses, often with a choice of sailing single-handed or in a bigger boat with an instructor. Most courses offer a combination of on-the-water training and classroom sessions to enable you to understand the technical side of sailing, too.

Sailing School

Sailing centers affiliated to US SAILING (the National Governing Body of Sailing in the U.S.A.) are found along the coasts and at lakes and reservoirs. These schools offer a safe introduction to sailing with lessons on land and on water. After a one-day session, you may be ready to sail a boat on your own!

Sailing Equipment

You will need a boat and some specialized gear, but at first, you should be able to borrow everything from your sailing center or school. There are technical names for each part of the boat, and it is important to know what these are when you are on the water.

Mainsail *The largest sail on the boat, attached to the boom and mast.*

Mast *The vertical pole that holds up the sail.*

Mainsheet *The rope used to pull in the mainsail.*

Jib *The smaller sail at the front of the boat. These only feature on double-handed boats.*

Boom *The horizontal pole that is attached to the bottom of the mainsail.*

Painter *The rope used to secure the boat to the land.*

Bow *The front of the boat.*

Hull *The main body of the boat.*

Daggerboard *This helps to steer and balance the boat by moving up and down into and out of the water.*

What to Wear

Sailing gear ensures you stay safe and comfortable on the water. As you become more interested in sailing, you may want to replace items borrowed from the sailing center by buying your own.

Life jacket *The most important piece of equipment for sailing. Made from spongy foam, it will help you to float straight back up to the surface if you fall in or capsize.*

Gloves *These keep your hands warm and protect them from blisters when you are pulling ropes around the boat. They are normally made from a stretchy material with strong, protective fabric across the palms.*

Wetsuit *This tight-fitting suit goes on straight over your swimsuit, and is designed to let you get soaking wet without getting cold. The material allows water to seep in, holding it next to your skin to warm it up, and preventing more cold water from rushing in.*

Boots *These are made from the same material as the wetsuit. It is important to wear proper sailing boots, because they allow your feet to get wet without getting cold, and protect your toes and the soles of your feet from getting injured on the boat.*

Tiller *This steers the boat.*

Rudder *This is attached to the tiller and controls the direction of the boat.*

Stern *The back of the boat.*

Safety First

If you fall overboard, you do not have time to react as quickly as your buoyancy aid will, even if you are a strong swimmer. But your buoyancy aid needs to be a snug fit. If it's too big, it will float up over your head and not be effective. To check it's a good fit, make sure it will support your body weight. If you can pull it over your head, you need to tighten up the fastenings or wear a smaller size.

11

Understanding the Wind

Getting to grips with wind direction is vital when learning to sail. When you are sailing, you need to angle the sails in different ways depending on the wind and the direction you want to travel in.

Moving with the Wind

When the wind hits the sail, it has the effect of pushing it over, as it would any other object. But thanks to the balance offered by the daggerboard and rudder, it is kept slightly more balanced. By leaning your weight out over the side of the boat, you can balance out this pushing effect. By doing this, you keep the boat upright, and let the power of the wind propel the boat forward.

Wind Direction

Look at a flag to find out the direction that the wind is blowing in. You cannot sail directly into the wind, so this angle (the angle that the flag is pointing in) will be one you need to avoid on the water. This is the **no-go zone**.

wind direction

Close-Hauled

Close-hauled is the closest you can get to sailing directly into the wind. If you want to sail to a point in the direction the wind is blowing in, you will be able to tightly zigzag your way almost directly toward it. To keep the boat balanced correctly, you will also need to have your **daggerboard** down as far as possible while you sit up on the side of the boat.

For close-hauled sailing, your mainsail should be pulled in as far as possible to catch as much wind as you can.

wind directi

sailing direction

Beam Reach

A **beam reach** is when the wind is blowing straight onto the side of the sail. If you want to sail in a forward direction, you should be able to do this without having to shift direction or zigzag toward it. This is the easiest and fastest way of sailing. You should usually be sitting out on the side of the boat, but you won't have to work as hard as you do when sailing close-hauled.

To go as fast as possible on a beam reach, the sail needs to be pulled in about halfway, and the daggerboard should also be raised halfway up.

wind direction

sailing direction

Training Run

A **training run** is where you are literally "running away from the wind." As well as letting the sails all the way out, you will also need to raise the daggerboard almost completely up.

On a training run, the wind blows over the back of the boat. You need to have the sail as far out as possible to catch the wind and be dragged forward.

Keep in Control

When you sail too close to the wind, your sails will lose power and start flapping, slowing you down and maybe even causing you to stop moving completely. Sailing schools will often use the phrase: "A flappy sail is an unhappy sail. Pull it in and make it grin!" to help remind you to keep your sail pulled in and as filled as possible.

wind direction

sailing direction

Getting Afloat

Each time you want to go sailing, your boat needs to be rigged. Rigging is putting together all sails and equipment that are stored separately while the boat is ashore.

Rigging

All boats are different when it comes to **rigging**, but there are a few things you should always check. Before putting up the sail, make sure the boat is "head to wind," which means that the front of the boat is pointing in the direction the wind is coming from.

While ashore, you should hoist the mainsail and attach the rudder and tiller, to prepare as far as possible before the boat enters the water. Make sure that the mainsheet has a knot at the end, which will stop it from whipping out of your reach while sailing.

With the sail up, the rudder attached, and the daggerboard in place, this boat is ready to sail.

Safety Checks

To avoid any accidents on the water, check that all the rigging ropes are stored tidily. Getting a foot or arm tangled in ropes is dangerous—so stay alert!

Launching

Once your boat is rigged then you are ready to launch the boat into the water. Keep the boat head to wind to make sure that it does not sail away while you are still on land. Roll the dolly down the beach or slipway until the boat floats up on the water. Secure the boat by tying it to the side of the slipway or ask a friend to hold the painter while you return the dolly to a safe spot on the land. When you are ready to set off, simply untie the painter and push yourself away from the shore.

Getting Afloat

As you leave the shore, sit on the side of the hull and face forward. Keep an eye out for any other boats in the area. Remember to tuck your feet under the **toe straps**, since this will prevent you from falling backward out of the boat.

Aim to keep the boat facing into the wind as you walk toward the water.

Lower the dolly onto the water until the boat floats.

Hold the mainsheet with your "front" hand and the tiller with your "back" hand.

Get a friend to hold the painter while you return the dolly to a safe place onshore.

As the helm of a single-handed boat, you will be in charge of the mainsail, daggerboard, and tiller. The most efficient way to position yourself in the boat is to hold the tiller and steer with your hand nearest to the back of the boat. This means your "front" hand is able to control the mainsail and daggerboard, and allows you to sit facing forward in a comfortable way.

Changing Direction

Sailing in a straight line is easy, but learning to change direction while sailing is more of a challenge. As you alter the angle of the boat toward the wind, your sail will automatically move with it, so you need to make sure you know how to adjust the positioning of the sail to keep your speed up.

Using the sail and tiller, you can turn your boat in any direction.

If you are sailing in one direction and want to turn around and sail the opposite way, you have two options for changing direction—**tacking** and **jibing**.

Tacking means turning a boat across the wind, with the wind blowing toward the front of the boat at all times. Jibing is when you change direction with the wind blowing onto the back of the boat.

To Tack or to Jibe?

If you are sailing close-hauled (roughly in the direction of the wind), you will need to remain as close-hauled as you can. To do this you will need to tack, since you want to keep pointing toward the wind. Tacking will move the boom from one side of the boat to the other, allowing the mainsail to fill up with wind again on the other side of the boat. This allows you to sail in a zigzag pattern.

*Changing direction, such as moving around a **mark**, requires you to pull in the sail and steer around with the tiller.*

Once the sail has swapped sides, you need to move across the boat and rearrange your ropes, ready to sail away.

The Main Differences

Tacking is the slowest and most steady way to change direction, since the bow of the boat moves through the wind, de-powering the sail and staying controllable. Since jibing moves the stern of the boat through the wind, there is always wind in the sails, making it much quicker than tacking.

To change direction when you are downwind (when the wind is behind you), you have two options. One is to pull the sail in tight, which will automatically pull your boat in one direction. The other is to jibe, where the stern will move across the wind and the boom will cross to the other side of the boat, letting you sail in the opposite direction.

Making a Turn

Tacking and jibing require slightly different movements but otherwise are quite similar. By following a simple step-by-step process, you will be able to see just how easy it is.

First check the surrounding area for other boats. Then prepare to move into the center of the boat.

Preparation

Hold the tiller in your "back" hand and the mainsheet in your "front" hand since this will help you stay in control. Ensure that the mainsheet is running freely and is not going to get caught as the sail moves across the boat. Look around to make sure you are clear to make the move.

Wait for the sail to move across and be prepared to duck under the boom.

Step-by-Step Tacking

1 Bring your body weight closer into the boat. If you have been sitting right on the edge, move farther into the center and slowly let the sail out.

2 Push the tiller as far away from you as possible and the boat will start to move into the wind. As the sail heads into the wind, it will move into the center of the boat and lose power. Duck under the boom and cross to the other side of the boat.

3 Once you are on the other side of the boat, straighten up the tiller to head in the right direction and pull the sail back in. Swap your hands so that your "back" hand is holding the tiller again, and your "front" hand is holding the mainsheet.

Once on the other side of the boat, "swap" hands so that your "back" hand is holding the tiller.

Jibing is similar to tacking, you just turn the boat in the opposite direction.

Step-by-Step Jibing

1 Move into the center of the boat and bring the tiller close to you.

2 The boom will begin to move slowly into the center of the boat.

3 Duck under the boom—it will move across the boat very quickly, as the wind moves to the other side of the sail.

4 Once the wind crosses the center of the boat, move to the other side of the boat and straighten up your steering to point in the right direction.

5 Swap your hands so that your "back" hand is controlling the tiller and your "front" hand is holding the mainsheet.

Communication Is the Key!

Jibing and tacking involve a lot of movement around the boat, so everyone needs to know what is going to happen. If sailing single-handed, make sure you are prepared before making a turn. If sailing double-handed, be sure to let your crew know when you are making a turn so they can prepare the ropes. The helm needs to shout when they start the turn, so the crew can make sure they avoid the boom and move across the boat at the right time.

in Deep Water!

Sailing boats keep their balance by the body weight of the sailors and the force of the wind in the sails. If your boat isn't balanced, you may capsize and it's essential to know what to do in this case. It's best to practice this drill before you actually have to use it!

Avoiding a Capsize

The best way to avoid capsizing is to act quickly when the boat begins to lean toward the water, or heel over. To prevent a full capsize there are two things you should do. First, lean as far out of the boat as possible, using the toe straps to keep you secure. You can also let out the sail slightly to spill some of the wind and regain your control.

If your boat capsizes and you cannot correct it, you should stay with the boat rather than try to swim to shore. You are more likely to be noticed by someone who can help.

Step-by-Step Capsize Recovery

If you do capsize, don't panic. Here are the steps to take to right yourself when your sail hits the water:

Make sure that you are free of all ropes and fittings. Swim to the inside of the boat and push the daggerboard all the way down.

Swim around to the underside of the boat and put your weight on the daggerboard. In strong winds or with heavy boats, you might need to climb up and stand on it to get enough weight to pull it up.

Use your weight to pull the boat upright.

As the boat rights itself, pull yourself into the hull.

Once back on board, untangle ropes, check that the rudder and tiller are still in place, and bail out any water in the bottom of the boat.

Turning Turtle

Although many boats have floats to prevent them from capsizing in strong winds and currents, there is a danger that a capsized boat will completely turn over, leaving the mast pointing directly downward into the water. This is known as "turning turtle," and is a little harder to correct than a simple capsize, although you should react in the same way. In this case, get hold of the mainsheet and use it to help pull the sail to the surface while you lean on the daggerboard as hard as possible.

The Next Step

Once you are happy with the basics of sailing, there are many more elements to try out to keep you on your toes, from double-handed sailing to trapezing, and even adding more sails to the challenge.

Trapezing allows you to use all your body weight to balance the boat.

Trapezing

Leaning out of the boat as far as possible lets you keep the sail pulled farther in and catch as much wind as you can, making you sail faster. **Trapezing** enables you to lean out even farther, letting you go even faster without losing control of the boat.

A trapeze is a harness that is attached to the boat by wires and enables the crew members to lean out of the boat to balance it. The trapeze itself is a stretch of elastic that runs from the top of the mast to the hull of the boat. Once you have hooked onto the trapeze, you can stand on the side of the boat and lean out as far as you can, using the mainsheet to help you stay stable.

The trapeze harness has straps over the shoulders and around the waist, joining with a hook in the middle.

A trapeze harness is worn underneath your life jacket.

Spinnakers

Certain types of boats also have an extra sail called a **spinnaker**. This is used when you are sailing downwind, since it is designed to balloon with the wind and pull you along, but cannot be pulled in tight like the mainsail.

You pull on the spinnaker halyard (a rope that runs up the mast) to hoist the sail, and then use a pole to keep it sticking as far out of the boat as possible. By tweaking the spinnaker **sheets**, you are then able to make sure the sail gets as full as possible. Once you are ready to change direction again, simply release the spinnaker halyard and drop the sail back into the pocket that it is stored in when not in use.

The spinnaker is an extra sail that is held out with a pole at the front of the boat.

23

On the Open Water

Once you have learned the basics of sailing through a US SAILING approved center, you may have the desire to get out on the open water. Proper planning for this kind of trip is essential, as is making sure you have all the necessary equipment in case of a sudden change in weather.

Day Cruising

Although a lot of sailors enjoy the thrill of high-powered racing, if you are not interested in going as fast as possible, then dinghy cruising is a great alternative. Rather than rushing around on the water, cruising is a great way to spend a leisurely day exploring the outdoors. You could pack a picnic and go on a family adventure to a beach that cannot be reached by car, or you could go for a short sail to a local sandy beach for ice cream. The possibilities are endless.

What to Take

Although you need to be prepared for every trip you take on the water, these new and exciting adventures require a little more planning and some extra supplies. You need to make sure that you have all the equipment onboard that you might need in an emergency.

Extra food and water *Sailing is very physical, so you need to make sure that you keep your energy levels up by having some healthy snacks on board and plenty of water in case it gets hot.*

Emergency cell phone It is important to have a cell phone with you so you can keep in contact with people onshore at all times. It is also a good idea to have some money in case you need to buy emergency supplies.

Sun protection The sun is even stronger when you are on the water so it is important to keep reapplying sunblock, even when the sun is not shining.

Personal medication In case you end up on the water for longer than you originally planned, it's best to take any personal medication with you, along with a first-aid kit.

Spare sweater The wind can be very cold on the open water, so an extra sweater or fleece jacket will keep you warm.

Sun hat Protect your eyes and face from the sun and wind with a peaked cap.

Knitted hat Heat leaves your body quickest through your head, so on cold days pack a knitted hat.

Towel A spare towel is always a good idea for splashes or even capsizes.

Competition Racing

Once you are skilled and confident on the water, why not try out dinghy racing? Sailing is a competitive sport at many levels, from races at your local sailing club to Olympic and Paralympic events.

How Racing Works

For racing, you need to be in complete control of your boat and understand the rules, so it's a good idea to take an initial course of lessons on racing with a qualified instructor. This will get you used to how dinghy racing works, explain the rules that will help you avoid a collision, and give you tips on going as fast as possible around the course.

Racing events such as this **regatta** can be very busy, so it is vital you know all the rules of the event.

Junior Racing

The best way to get involved in junior racing is at your local sailing club. This will usually be open for children under the age of 18, and will often include race training sessions and classes to help you improve your skills as you gain confidence.

Rules and Regulations

There are plenty of racing rules, but you only need a few to get started. The best way to learn is to watch more capable racers and to see how they act at different points around the course.

The most basic and important rule is that the boat on **starboard tack** is always in the right. Being on starboard tack means that your sail is on the left-hand side of your boat and you are sitting on the right-hand side. If your sail is on the right and you are sitting on the left, then you are on **port tack**, and you have to keep out of the way of anyone sailing on starboard. You will soon gather handy rules such as these, helping you to become competitive on the racing course.

This boat is sailing on port tack, and so will have to keep out of the way of any oncoming boats.

Sailing on starboard tack means you have the right of way over oncoming boats.

Understanding the Course

Before you start a race, you will have a **briefing** onshore, in which someone will explain where the course is (usually marked out by big, floating **buoys** on the water), in what order you need to go around the marks, and on what side of your boat you need to pass by the mark. This is also a chance to ask questions and to get some helpful advice. Everyone is a learner sometime, and other sailors will be happy to help and encourage you.

Sailing Challenges!

After you have had your first dinghy sailing experiences, you will want to get involved in all kinds of other challenges, and luckily there are lots out there for you to choose from!

Some larger sailing boats have sleeping quarters and are perfect for family adventures!

Camping on Water!

Dinghy sailing is unique because it lets you get to beaches and destinations that you cannot reach by car or bike. This makes it perfect for going on adventures to discover new places and find the perfect picnic spot. Some larger dinghies have room to set up a bed inside, so you can even spend the night on board. It's a little like camping—but on the water. Other, larger styles of boat are perfect for families, for day trips, or for longer.

Larger yachts on the open water require bigger teams to handle them.

Yachting Challenges

Yachts are just the same as dinghies, except much bigger, and often with an inside section that has beds and a kitchen area. This means that you can stay onboard for much longer periods of time, making them perfect for week-long trips and longer journeys abroad. Up to 20 people are needed to sail some yachts, and everyone on board has an important job to do, making sure the boat sails safely and as quickly as possible. Yacht racing is a very popular, exhilarating sport that is competitive at every level.

Great Expeditions

The bigger the boat you sail, the farther away from home you can go. While you can sail near the shore in your dinghy, some bigger boats regularly make trips around the globe, spending months at sea and experiencing some of the most extreme conditions on Earth. This may not be something you can tackle right away, but it would be an amazing dream to have for the future...

Around the World

There is no minimum age requirement for sailing. On August 27, 2009, 17-year-old Mike Perham became the youngest person to sail around the world in a yacht. Although he met his dad in a couple of countries along the way, he sailed across the oceans all on his own.

Glossary

Beam reach Sailing at a 90-degree angle to the wind.

Briefing The meeting before a sailing race where you are told about the course and when you need to start racing.

Buoy A floating ball that marks out the course or an area of water.

Close-hauled Sailing as close to the wind as possible.

Crew The sailor who controls the jib but does not steer the boat.

Daggerboard This moves directly up and down, into and out of the water, and helps steer the boat and adds balance.

Dinghy A small, open-top boat, often only designed for one sailor at a time.

Helm The sailor controlling the rudder and mainsail.

Jibing To change direction with the wind over the back of the boat.

Launch Removing the boat from its trailer and getting it afloat, ready to sail.

Mark The buoys that identify the route you have to race.

No-go zone The direction the wind is blowing from. It is not possible to sail in this direction.

Port tack This is when you are sailing with the sail on the right-hand side of the boat.

Recover After a capsize, recovery is the process of correcting the boat so that it is ready to sail again. It can also simply mean to remove the boat from the water.

Regatta A big racing event.

Rigging The name for the sails and ropes, but it is also the act of setting up the boat before you sail.

Rudder This is attached to the tiller and controls the direction of the boat.

Sheets In sailing, these are ropes, lines, or cables.

Spinnaker A extra sail that is used when sailing downwind.

Starboard tack This is when you are sailing with the sail on the left-hand side of the boat.

Tacking To change direction by moving through the wind.

Toe straps These are used to hook your feet under when you are sitting on the side of the boat.

Trailer A metal frame with wheels used to store and move the boat when on land.

Training run Sailing with the wind behind you.

Trapezing A harness attached to a wire at the top of the mast, allowing a sailor to get their body weight over the side of the boat.

Yacht A large boat, generally with an indoor section and space for a crew of three or more.

Books to Read

Adventure on the High Sea!
by Susan Barry Blair
(Xlibris Corporation, 2006)

The Olympic Sports: Rowing, Sailing,
*   and Other Sports on the Water*
by Jason Page
(Crabtree Publishing, 2008)

The Winner's Guide to Optimistic Sailing
by Gary Jobson
(Ragged Mountain Press, 2004)

Web Sites

Due to the changing nature of Internet links, PowerKids Press has developed an online list of Web sites related to the subject of this book. This site is updated regularly. Please use this link to access this list:
http://www.powerkidslinks.com/go/sailing

index

Ainslie, Ben 7

balance 6, 7, 10, 12,
    20, 22, 23
beam reach 13, 30
boat 4, 5, 6, 7, 8, 9, 10,
    11, 12, 13, 14, 15, 16,
    17, 18, 19, 20, 21, 22,
    23, 26, 27, 28, 29
    dinghy 5, 7, 24, 26,
        28, 29, 30
    double-handed 5, 8,
        10, 19, 22
    main parts 10, 11
    single-handed 5, 8,
        9, 15, 19
    yacht 5, 29, 30
boom 10, 17, 18, 19
bow 10, 17

capsize 11, 20, 21, 25
close-hauled 12, 13, 17, 30
clothes 11, 25
club 6, 7, 8, 9, 26, 27
competitions 7, 26–27, 29
crew 5, 19, 23, 30

daggerboard 10, 12,
    13, 14, 15, 21, 30
direction 4, 5, 11, 12,
    13, 14, 16, 17, 18, 19, 23

equipment 9, 10–11,
    14, 24

fitness 7

helm 5, 15, 19, 30
hull 10, 15, 21, 23

instructor 8, 9, 26

jibing 16, 17, 18, 19, 30

learning 5, 8, 9, 12, 16, 27
life jacket 11, 23

mast 10, 21, 23
muscles 7

no-go zone 12, 30

ocean 4, 6, 29
Olympic Games 7, 26

Perham, Mike 29
port tack 27, 30
professionals 8

racing 4, 5, 7, 24, 26–27, 29
rigging 14, 15, 30
river 4, 5, 6
ropes 10, 11, 14, 15,
    17, 18, 19, 21, 23
    mainsheet 10, 14,
        15, 18, 19, 21, 23
    painter 10, 15
rudder 4, 11, 12, 14,
    21, 30
rules 26, 27

safety 8, 11, 14, 24, 25, 29
sail 4, 5, 7, 10, 12, 13,
    14, 15, 16, 17, 18, 19,
    20, 21, 22, 23, 27
    jib 10
    mainsail 10, 12, 14,
        15, 17, 23
    spinnaker 23, 30

sailing school 6, 9, 10,
    11, 13, 24
skills 6, 7, 27
speed 4, 5, 13, 16, 22,
    26, 29
starboard tack 27, 30
steering 4, 5, 9, 10, 11,
    15, 17, 19
stern 11, 17
swimming 8, 11, 20, 21

tacking 16, 17, 18, 19, 30
technique 8, 9, 12–13,
    14–15, 16–17, 18–19,
    20–21, 22–23
tiller 11, 14, 15, 16,
    17. 18, 19, 21
toe straps 15, 20, 30
trailer 5, 30
training 6, 9, 27
training run 13, 30
trapezing 22, 23, 30

US SAILING 9, 24

warming up 7
water 4, 5, 6, 7, 8, 9,
    10, 11, 12, 14, 15, 20,
    21, 24, 25, 26, 27, 28
weather 8, 24
wetsuit 11
wind 4, 8, 12, 13, 14,
    15, 16, 17, 18, 19, 20,
    21, 22, 23, 25